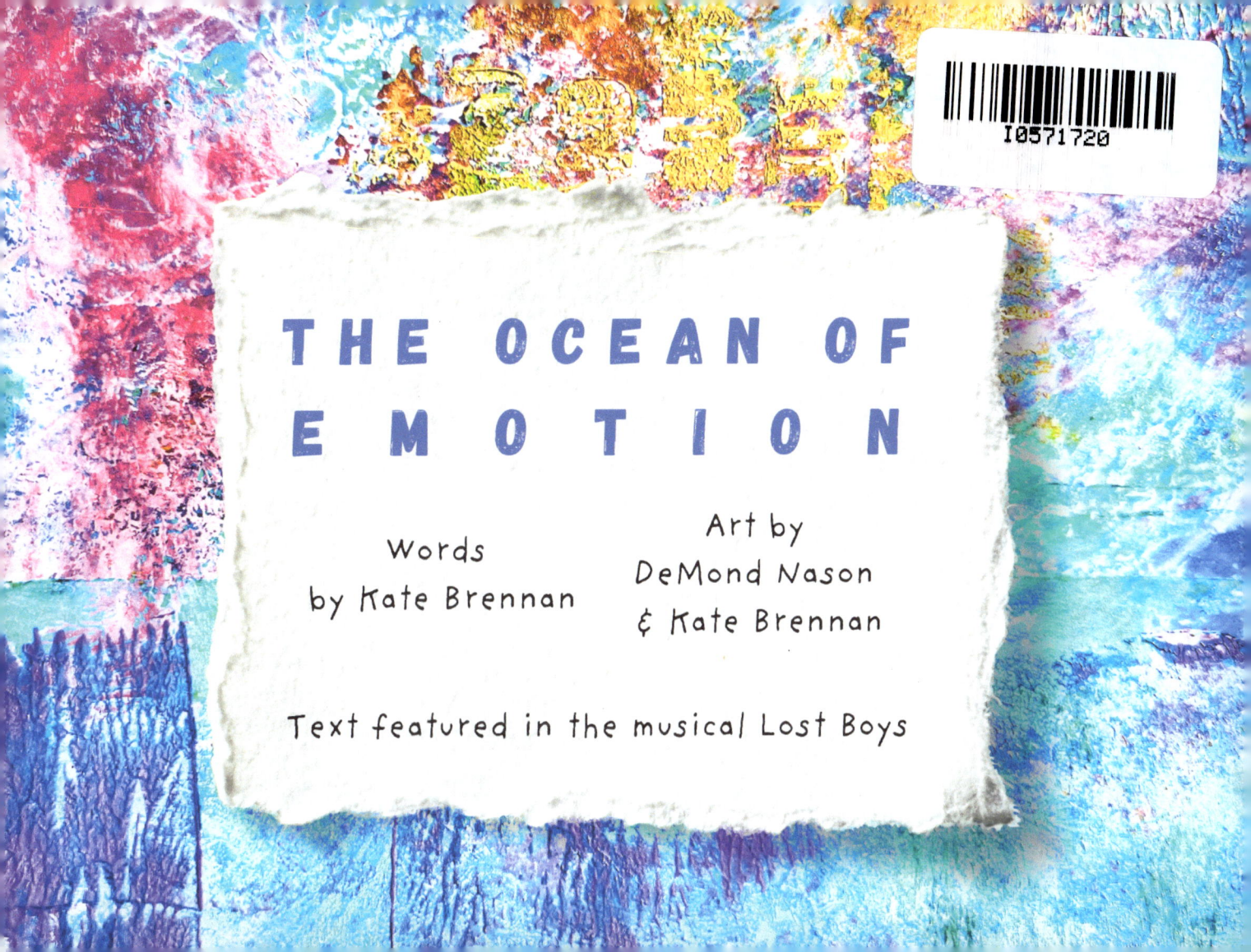

THE OCEAN OF EMOTION

Words
by Kate Brennan

Art by
DeMond Nason
& Kate Brennan

Text featured in the musical Lost Boys

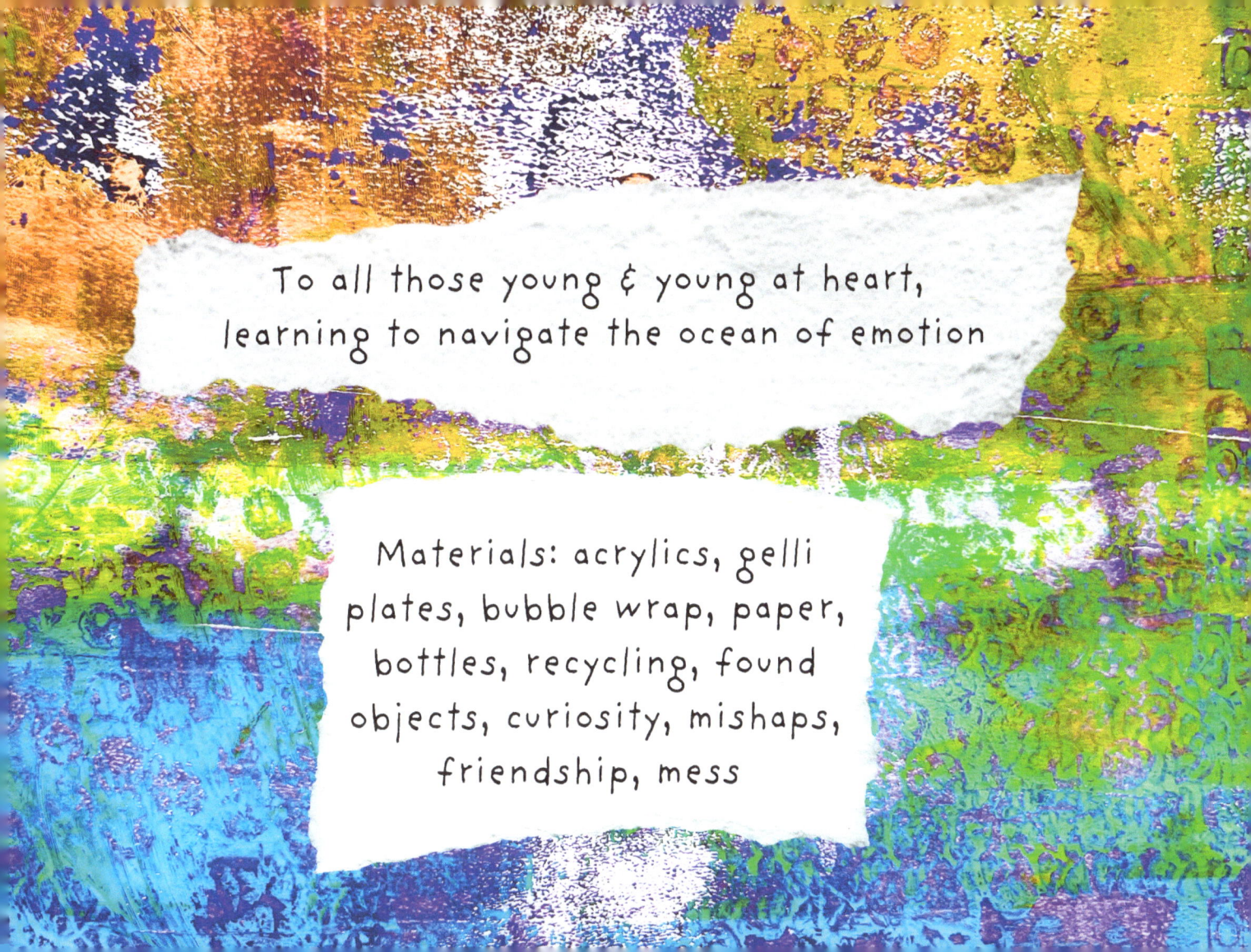

To all those young & young at heart,
learning to navigate the ocean of emotion

Materials: acrylics, gelli
plates, bubble wrap, paper,
bottles, recycling, found
objects, curiosity, mishaps,
friendship, mess

I have so many emotions
Churning inside
They manifest worlds
They turn like the tide

They help me to learn
And to share and to grow
Sometimes they come fast
Sometimes they leave slow

I'm happy and hangry
And silly and sad
Excited and frustrated
Jealous and mad

It's harder to cope
When I haven't had sleep
When I'm feeling stressed out
Or need something to eat

I can handle them better
When I breathe in deep
And feel where I am
And stand on my two feet

I feel cautious and anxious
Peaceful and proud
And I feel such relief
When I name them out loud

I am heavy exhausted

Weighed like a stone

Shrouded and lost

Adrift and alone

Sometimes I don't care much

Sometimes I feel bad

These are the moments

When I'm feeling

SAD

I am jagged and blurry
Confused, angry red

When effort and worry
Collide in my head

I am angular, pointy
Like teeth are serrated
These are the moments
When I feel

FRUSTRATED

I am cloudy and hazy
A gray fog descends
A tether that's frayed
And loose at both ends

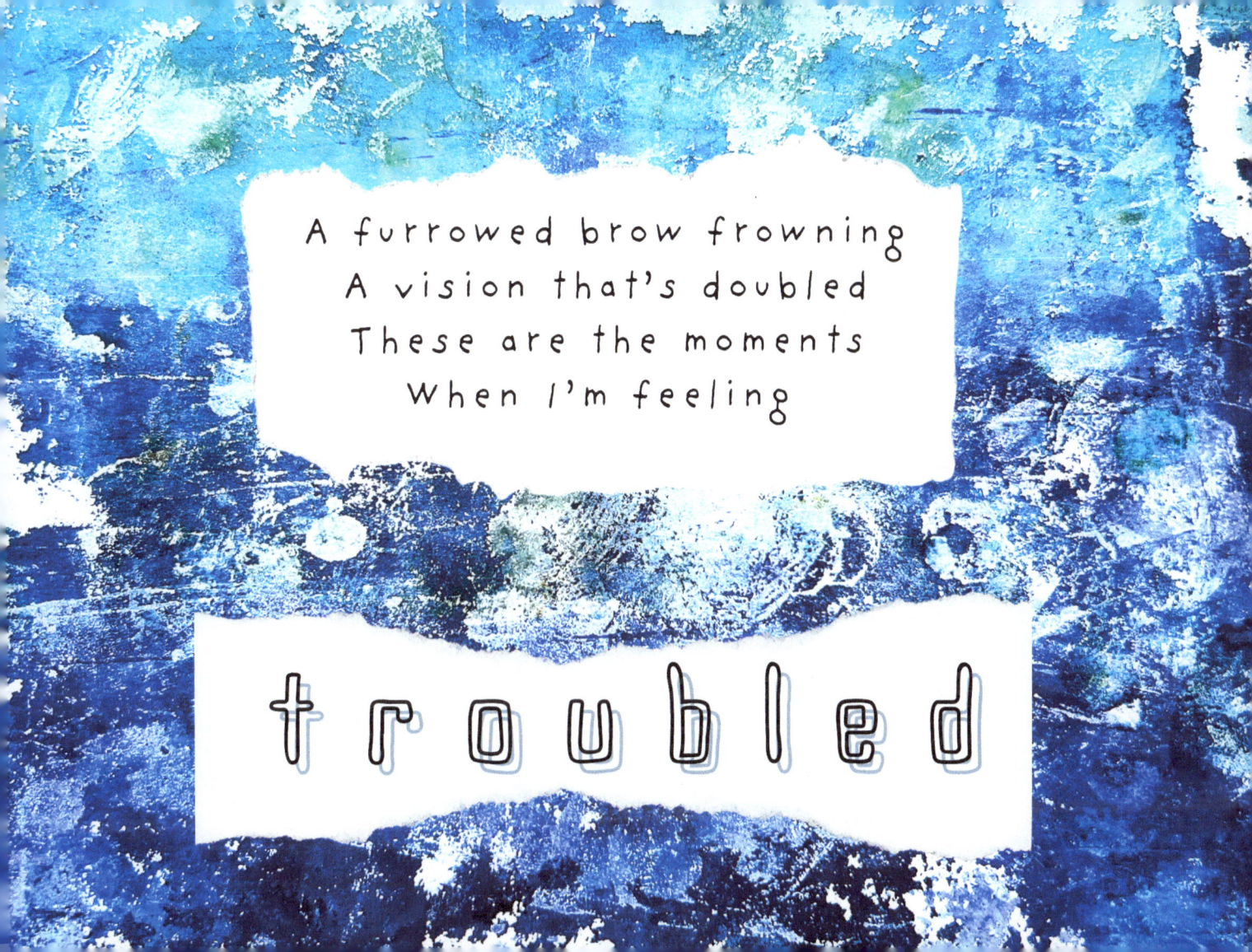

A furrowed brow frowning
A vision that's doubled
These are the moments
When I'm feeling

troubled

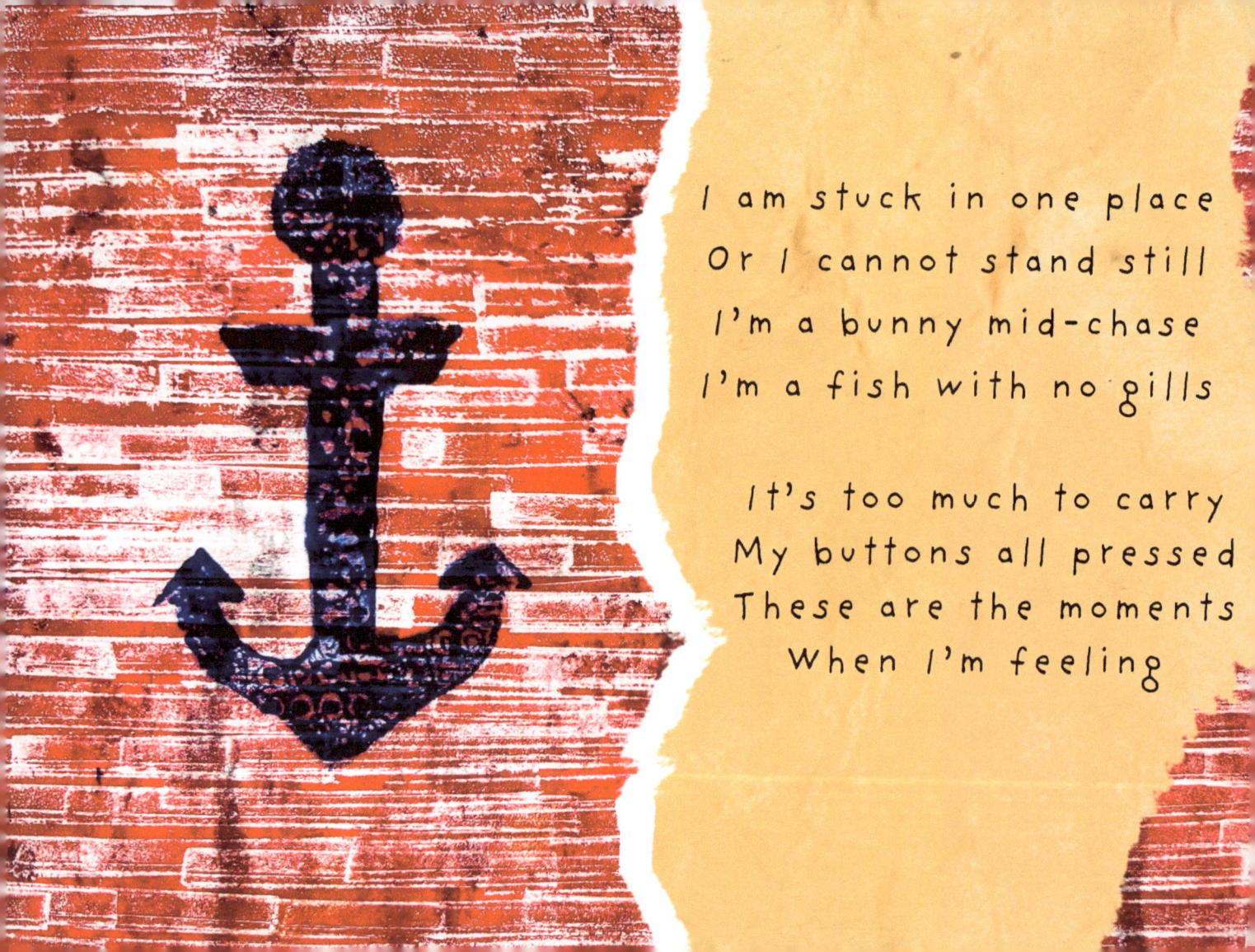

I am stuck in one place
Or I cannot stand still
I'm a bunny mid-chase
I'm a fish with no gills

It's too much to carry
My buttons all pressed
These are the moments
When I'm feeling

I'm the spacious
blue sky

I am green as
desire

I am light as a
snowflake

Courageous as
fire

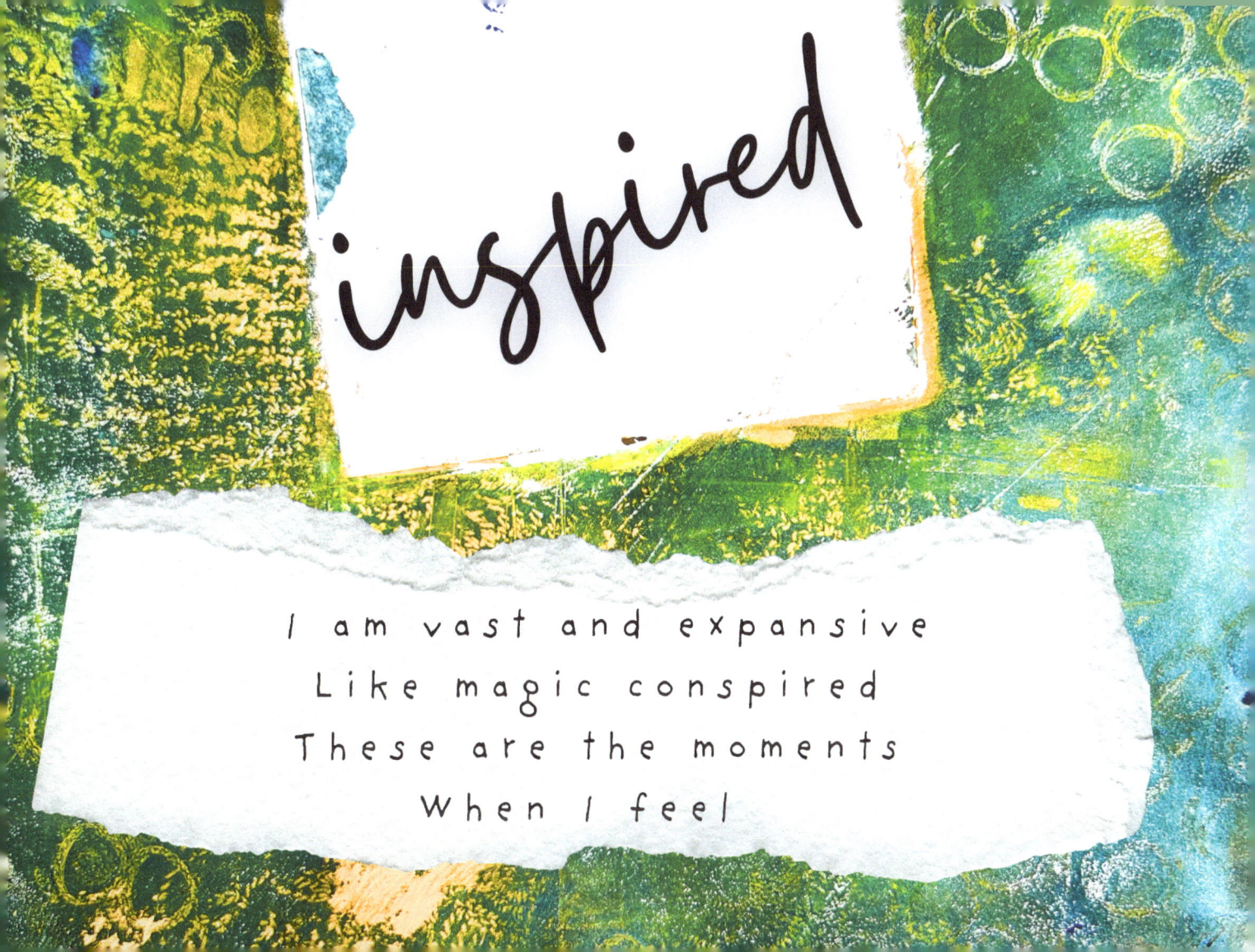

inspired

I am vast and expansive
Like magic conspired
These are the moments
When I feel

I'm an uneasy shaking
A leaf in the wind
A chestnut earthquaking
A top in a spin

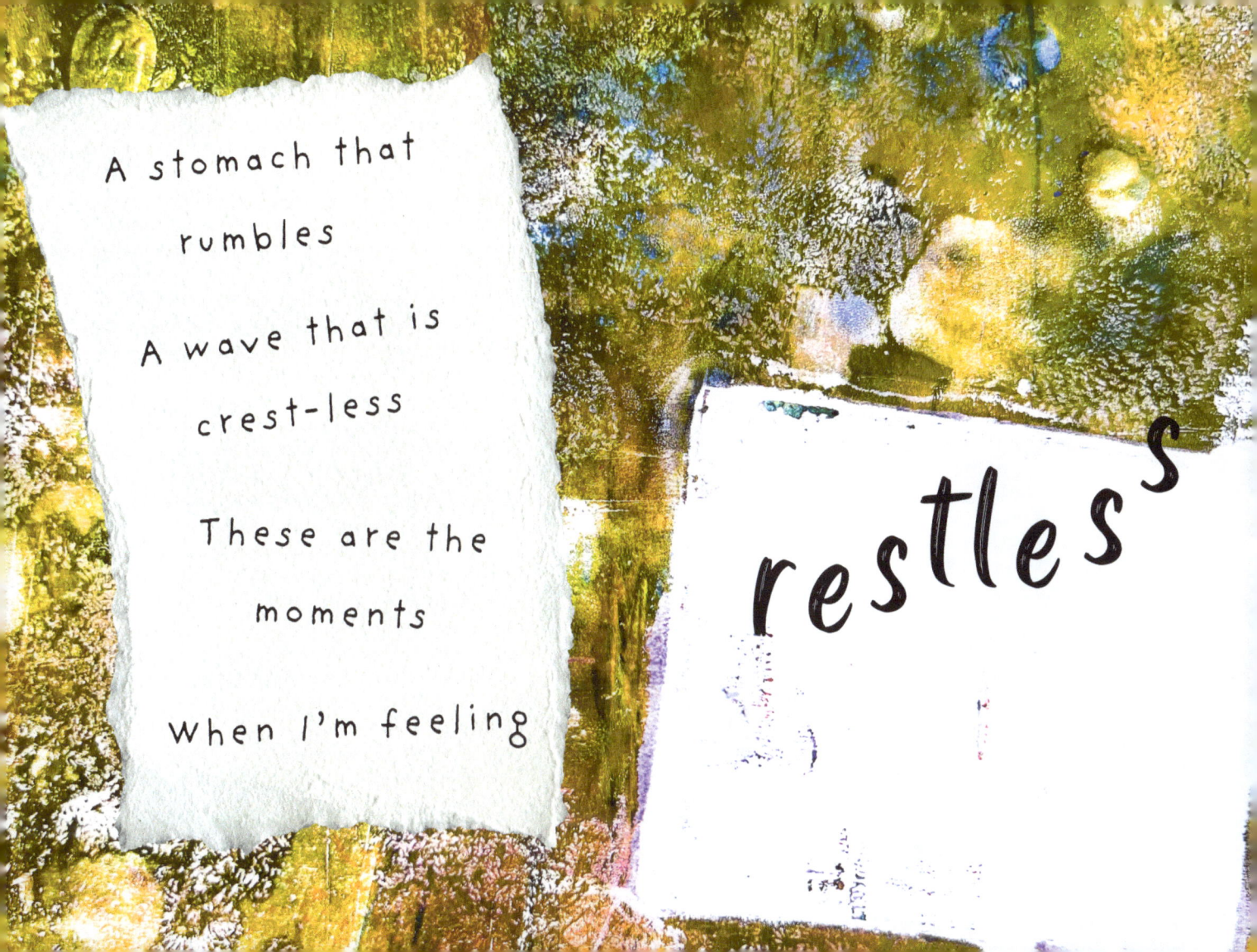

A stomach that rumbles

A wave that is crest-less

These are the moments

When I'm feeling

restless

I am open and easy
As gentle as air

Part strong
and part breezy
With compassion
and care

I'm receptive to others
And feel such release

These are the
moments
When I am at

peace

I feel nestled

inside

The coziest

bed

The world is so

wide

Inside of my

head

thought

I might seem distracted
Like I wander a lot
These are the moments
When I'm lost in

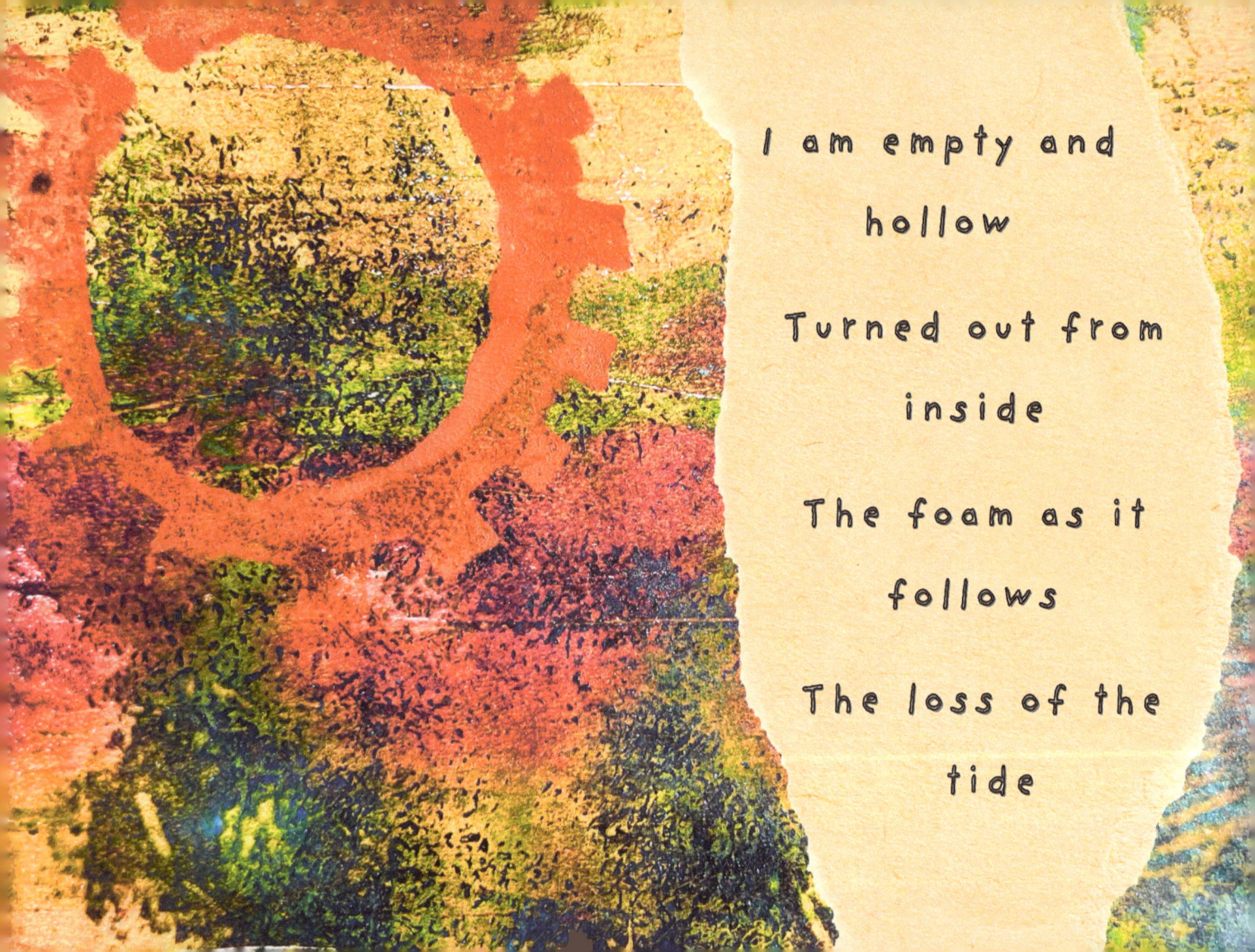

I am empty and hollow
Turned out from inside
The foam as it follows
The loss of the tide

I am running on fumes
On a motor that's strained
These are the moments
When I'm feeling

drained

I'm a dog on a run

Or a stalk sprouting tall

Flowers bent to the sun

Or a squirrel in the fall

I'm well-rested and eager
And just the right size
These are the moments
I feel

energized

I am volcanic eruption
An avalanche crash
An iceberg abruption
A hot lightning flash

An electric guitar
A bear trapped in a cage
These are the moments
When I'm feeling

I am tiptoeing wide-eyed
I am taut and aware
I see shadows on all sides
And ghosts in midair

frightened

I am tiny and quick
Every muscle is tightened
These are the moments
When I'm feeling

I'm a helium balloon

A mockingbird call

A beam from the moon

A shiny red ball

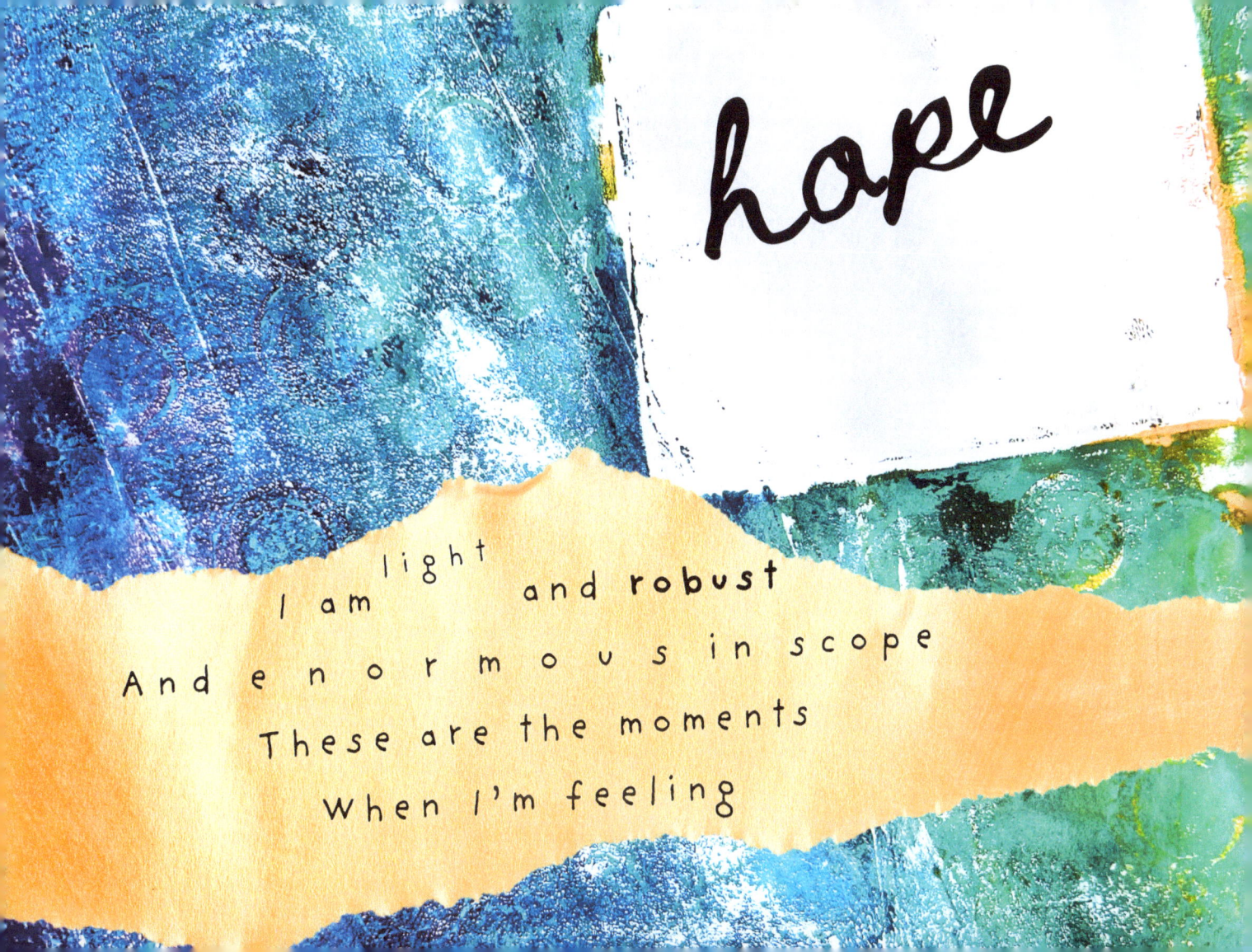

hope

I am light and **robust**
And e n o r m o u s in scope
These are the moments
When I'm feeling

I am yielding and
porous

A fish in the
sea

Kaleidoscopic
auroras

Blue
simplicity

The lines become blurry
Between the you that is me
These are the moments
I feel
empathy

I'm electric and buzzy
As high as the trees
Sweaty and fuzzy
A hive full of bees

I am orange
and scribbly
Pink bouncy
static
These are the
moments
I'm feeling

ecstatic

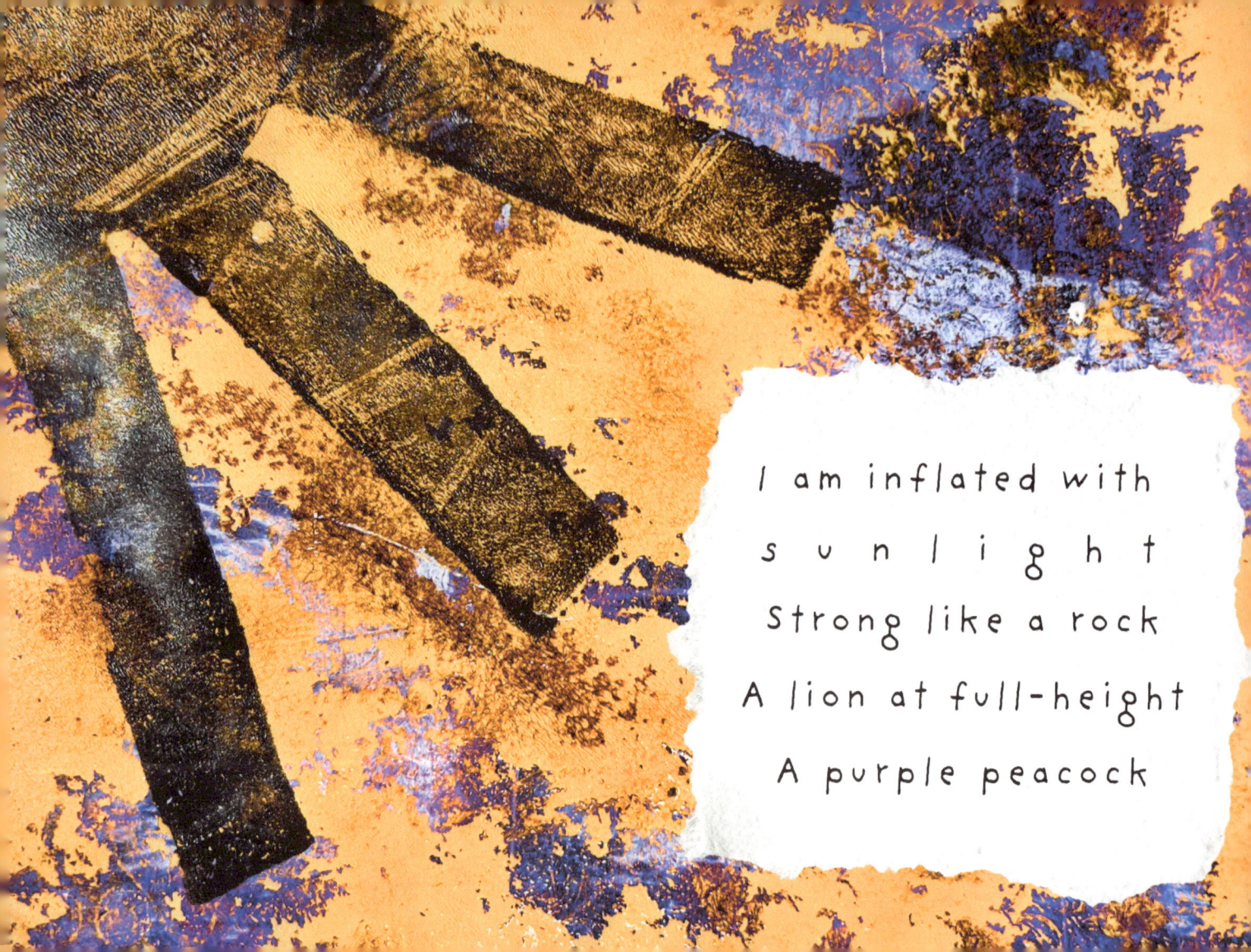

I am inflated with

s u n l i g h t

Strong like a rock

A lion at full-height

A purple peacock

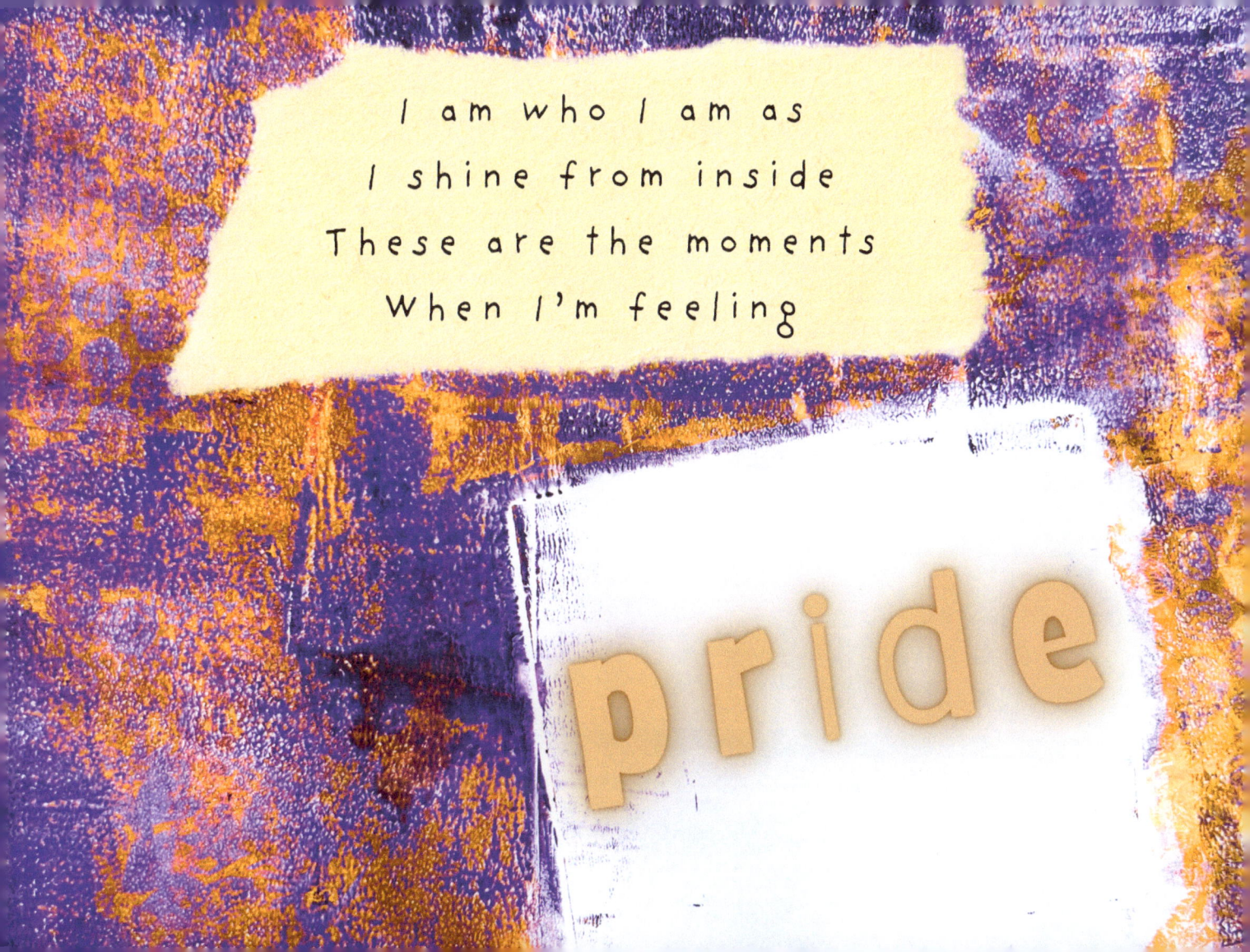

I am who I am as
I shine from inside
These are the moments
When I'm feeling

pride

But for all their strains

Now their music will guide me

These wild watercolors

Are the ocean inside me

www.ingramcontent.com/pod-product-compliance
Lightning Source LLC
Chambersburg PA
CBHW041614120626
46551CB00002B/447